Trumpet II in B♭

BRASS ON BROADWAY

arranged for brass quintet
by Bob Lowden

intermediate level

T0058439

THE CANADIAN BRASS

CANADIAN
BRASS
SERIES OF
COLLECTED QUINTETS

BROADWAY BABY
(From *FOLLIES*)

2nd TRUMPET

Words and Music by
Stephen Sondheim

Copyright © 1971 by Range Road Music Inc., Quartet Music Inc., Rilting Music, Inc. and Burthen Music Co., Inc.
This arrangement Copyright © 1989 by Range Road Music Inc., Quartet Music Inc., Rilting Music, Inc. and Burthen Music Co., Inc.
All rights administered by Herald Square Music, Inc.   International Copyright Secured   Made In U.S.A.
All Right Reserved   Used by Permission

COMEDY TONIGHT

From *A FUNNY THING HAPPENED ON THE WAY TO THE FORUM*

2nd TRUMPET

Words and Music by
Stephen Sondheim

Copyright ©1962 by Stephen Sondheim Burthen Music Co., Inc., owner of publication and allied rights
throughout the World (Chappell & Co. sole selling agent.)
This arrangement Copyright ©1989 by Burthen Music Co., Inc.
International Copyright Secured   ALL RIGHTS RESERVED   Printed in the U.S.A.
Unauthorized copying, arranging, adapting, recording or public performance is an infringement of copyright.
Infringers are liable under the Law.

GET ME TO THE CHURCH ON TIME
(From *My Fair Lady*)

2nd TRUMPET

Words by Alan Jay Lerner
Music by Frederick Loewe

Copyright © 1956 by Alan Jay Lerner and Frederick Loewe
This arrangement Copyright © 1989 by Alan Jay Lerner and Frederick Loewe
Chappell & Co. owner of publication and allied rights throughout the World.
International Copyright Secured   ALL RIGHTS RESERVED   Printed in the U.S.A.
Unauthorized copying, arranging, adapting, recording or public performance is an infringement of copyright.
Infringers are liable under the Law.

6

OL' MAN RIVER
(From *SHOW BOAT*)

2nd TRUMPET

Words by Oscar Hammerstein II
Music by Jerome Kern

Copyright © 1927 Polygram International Publishing, Inc. Copyright Renewed.
This arrangement Copyright © 1989 by Polygram International Publishing, Inc.
International Copyright Secured   Made in U.S.A.   All Rights Reserved

SUNRISE, SUNSET
(From *FIDDLER ON THE ROOF*)

2nd TRUMPET

Words by Sheldon Harnick
Music by Jerry Bock

Copyright ©1964 by Alley Music Corporation and Trio Music Company, Inc.
This arrangement Copyright ©1989 by Alley Music Corporation and Trio Music Company, Inc.
All rights administered by Hudson Bay Music, Inc.
International Copyright Secured   Made in U.S.A.   All Rights Reserved   Used by Permission

CANADIAN BRASS
SERIES OF COLLECTED QUINTETS

BRASS ON BROADWAY

arranged for brass quintet
by Bob Lowden

contents

Welcome to the *Canadian Brass Series of Collected Quintets*. In our work with students, for some time we have been aware of the need for more brass quintet music at easy and intermediate levels of difficulty. We are continually observing a kind of "Renaissance" in brass music, not only in audience responses to our quintet, but to all brass music in general. The brass quintet, as a chamber ensemble, seems to have become as standard a chamber combination as a string quartet. That could not have been said twenty-five years ago. Brass quintets are popping up everywhere — professional quintets, junior and senior high school ensembles, college and university groups, and amateur quintets of adult players.

We have carefully chosen the literature for these collected quintets, and closely supervised the arrangements. Our aim was to retain a Canadian Brass flavor to each arrangement, and create attractive repertory designed so that any brass quintet can play it with satisfying results. We've often remarked to one another that we certainly wish that we'd had quintet arrangements like these when we were students!

Happy playing to you and your quintet.

— THE CANADIAN BRASS

U.S. $8.99

ISBN-13: 978-1-4584-0167-0

Distributed By

HAL•LEONARD® CORPORATION
7777 W. BLUEMOUND RD. P.O. BOX 13819 MILWAUKEE, WI 53213

HL50488779